THE WONDERFUL WORLD OF QUADCOPTERS AND DRONES

28 Creative Uses for Recreation and Business

Contents

Introduction

S tatus quos are made to be broken. – Ray Davis

Deep in lush, endangered rainforests, camera-equipped quadcopters are recording the geography of the land on a mission that will result in the creation of 3D maps of large sections of land.

A project of "Drones for Good," these quadcopters are trying to save these precious wild habitats.

Once the maps are completed, specially constructed drones filled with seed pods will be deployed. The pods will be strategically opened for germination in an amazing endeavor that will see a projected one billion trees planted each year.

This is just one brilliant example of the way quadcopters, small remote-controlled helicopters with four rotors, are being used to change our world forever.

As a mental health professional with a special interest in unmanned aerial vehicles (UAVs) such as quadcopters and drones, this is the latest in my series of books about these fascinating pieces of technology and how they impact our society.

This book is on one level a guide to exploring the many uses of quadcopters. But on another level, it is an acknowledgment of how this new technology is gradually opening up whole new areas of exploration and scientific possibilities on our planet.

UAVs are undoubtedly one of the fastest growing technology trends to impact all areas of industry, leisure and overall society. Even Martha Stewart, the voice of the inspired living set, felt so passionate about them that she was moved to write an article called "Why I Love My Drone" in the July, 2014, edition of *Time* magazine.

This growing popularity is accompanied by a mixture of intrigue and fascination from those who use them or see their tremendous potential. It is also coupled with a measure of controversy over moral and ethical privacy issues and regulation challenges.

I expect you are aware of the popularity of the "selfie" where a person takes a photo of themselves with their camera phone and then posts it on Facebook. Now a whole new group of creative people have started to take "dronies," which are pictures of themselves taken from 100 feet above.

Already drones have revolutionized the film industry, and missions once considered pure science fiction are now everyday realities for military and security operations. Currently more than 50 countries around the world use some form of UAVs for policing purposes.

Our industries are constantly seeking ways this technology can be useful in their unending quest for further efficiencies. In 2013, for example, Amazon began testing UAVs as a potential method of delivering packages.

Quadcopters are also adding to the effectiveness of search and rescue efforts in remote areas and are even helping to gain valuable information about forest fires and agricultural crops.

They are also fun.

It wasn't until I started using them at home that I realized their personal potential. For example, once I sent my children a snack in the evening with my quadcopter. Another time I was upstairs and my wife realized she had forgotten her car keys just as she was about to go out. I sent her keys down to her with my quadcopter.

I began taking it to family picnics to record little videos, and in a very short time I realized I was becoming quite passionate about its potential to add a new dimension to my own life.

In this guide, I want to share some knowledge and ideas with you about introducing quadcopters in your own life as well as considering their impact on the larger sectors of society. I hope after reading this that you will embrace remote controlled drones as fun and useful technology.

You will learn about the impact of camera-carrying quadcopters on photography and filmmaking, allowing us to obtain a new perspective on our world. We will explore their use in the real estate industry and in the world of package delivery.

We will see how they are being used by the military and police forces around the world to help keep us safe.

We will also explore how they are changing the world as we know it in so many other areas of our life, from the construction of homes and buildings to education, farming and fishing.

We will also look at the joyful contribution they make to the fine art of having fun and discuss some of the recreational games involving quadcopters.

In each of these fields, we will look at both the recreational and commercial uses and open minds to how many different things they can do.

For example, if you love to go fishing, I will show you how to use your RC drone to locate fish, find the right fishing spot and capture beautiful pictures of the fish you catch.

Most of all, you will learn how quadcopters can change the perspectives from which you can view the world, and through that process broaden your experiences and add new depth and dimension to them. Once again we are discovering that the world is not flat.

How to Explore with Federal Aviation Authority (FAA) Approval

Before you begin using your quadcopter for any of the 10 applications discussed in this guide, please know there are certain rules and regulations you need to follow. These rules have not been made to limit your fun with RC drones, but to ensure everyone has a good time without endangering the safety of others. As such, here is a closer look at what the United States Federal Aviation Authority (FAA) says about RC drones.

While the average hobbyist may see an RC drone as a regular toy, the FAA believes it is an aircraft and regardless of size, the responsibility to fly safely applies equally to manned and unmanned aircraft operations.

Model aircraft, which by the FAA definition includes RC drones used solely for recreational purposes, can be flown freely as long as seven basic rules are followed:

1. You must fly below 400 feet and stay clear of surrounding obstacles.

2. You must keep your drone within your visual line of sight at all times.

3. You must remain well clear of manned aircraft operations and not interfere with them in any way.

4. You must not fly within five miles of an airport unless you contact the airport and control tower before flying and receive permission.

5. You must never fly near or over people or stadiums.

6. You cannot fly any model aircraft that weighs more than 55 pounds.

7. You cannot fly in a careless or reckless manner. If caught, you will be fined for endangering people.

The FAA has teamed up with a number of model aircraft and RC drone clubs in the United States to promote a safety campaign called "Know Before You Fly." They urge clubs to help educate the public about using UAVs safely and responsibly.

You are encouraged to fly your drones within the perimeters of a model aircraft club and even in your backyard for personal enjoyment, as long as you are more than five miles from an airport and the quadcopter will not get entangled in wires or other impediments. You can also fly a drone as part of a safety lesson.

You cannot, under any circumstances as the law now stands, use your drone for commercial purposes without a license.

These are the general guidelines. But you should also be aware of two things: Certain agencies or industries have secured exceptions to these guidelines. Also, the guidelines with reference to commercial use are going to be changed soon.

For example, currently if you charged a client a fee to use your camera-carrying quadcopter to take aerial photographs of a wedding or real estate, you would likely get a cease-and-desist letter from the FAA and there is potential for legal action in some cases.

However, the FAA has just announced this year that it is introducing a new set of proposals that will continue to allow it to regulate drones, but will make adjustments to allow their commercial use to move forward.

The FAA outlined the proposed changes in a news release. There are seven main elements to the changes:

1. All UAVs that weigh less than 55 pounds and are travelling less than 100 miles per hour (87 knots) maximum speed are covered under the proposed regulations.

2. Operators of these UAVs will not need to possess an FAA airman certificate. However, they will have to pass an initial aeronautical knowledge test at an FAA-approved knowledge-testing center. That step is estimated to cost $300. When you go for your test, you will also be subjected to a security check.

3. You are not permitted to fly your UAV if you know you have any physical or mental condition that might interfere with its safe operation.

4. You can only fly your UAV in daylight hours where there is at least three miles of visibility and with clouds at or over 500 feet above ground level.

5. You will be allowed to fly in certain contained airspaces (Classes B,C, D and E) if you have prior air traffic control clearance.

6. All small UAVs must be registered, but will not require an FAA airworthiness certificate.

7. Specific commercial operations will be permitted including research and development uses, crop monitoring, educational uses, power-line and pipeline inspections in hilly or mountain-ous regions, antenna inspections, bridge inspections, aerial photography, aiding certain rescue operations and evaluations of wildlife nesting areas.

The FAA regulators say the knowledge test will have to be done every two years and you will need an "operator's certificate" for the drone you are flying. The UAV operator has to be at least 17 years of age.

All of these rules will be for businesses only, not for the hobbyists. But these are mentioned here so that you will know as you become more versed in the use of your quadcopter and you sense its commercial potential, you will know there are steps to take to use it to make money.

As mentioned earlier, there are also some exceptions and proposed exceptions to the current rules. For example, the proposed Colorado Drone Bill would require law enforcement agencies to have a warrant before using a drone in surveillance cases unless there is imminent threat to life or risk of a terrorist attack.

There is every sign that companies are poised to take advantage of the commercial aspects of drones as soon as they can legally do so. Publishing giant Amazon revealed as far back as 2013 that they hoped to use drones as a means of delivering packages.

Now that we have some understanding of the rules and regulations surrounding drone use, let's look at some ways your quadcopter can be used.

What Can RC Drones Be Used For?

Aerial Photography

Aerial photography has always been one of the most exciting artistic ventures in the world, dating back to 1858 when French balloonist and photographer Gaspard-Félix Tournachon took pictures from his hot air balloon. Slowly, the art evolved to kite photography where, as the description suggests, cameras were attached to kites.

Today some of the most stunning pictures of the Earth, cities, events, nightlife and entire landscapes are captured with aerial photography. For example, the symmetry of the Arc de Triomphe in Paris is evident with a single aerial shot, as is the beauty of New York's Central Park.

While aerial photography may enable you to capture some of the greatest images on earth, the process in the past was arduous and expensive. It required that you purchased an expensive camera with a rapid shutter to counter the motion blur caused by the movement of a helicopter, plane or hot air balloon. Moreover, if you booked these expensive modes of transportation on the wrong day and the weather and clouds did not cooperate, you could waste your investment and end up without the photos you wanted.

Thanks to RC drones, you can take stunning aerial photos when and wherever you want. Best of all, you do not need to hire a pricey helicopter, worry about hot air balloons or try to conquer your fear of heights to take a good photo. While you may not be able to fly thousands of feet into the air, with the right RC drone and camera, you can still capture magnificent photos.

Nature Photography

Capturing photographs of animals in their natural settings without disturbing them, filming fields of wildflowers or securing views of terrains that your feet cannot carry you to is all possible now with your quadcopter camera.

Where only the intrepid explorers could go before, the average person can now envision and secure with a mounted digital camera on a quadcopter.

Drones soar over heavily forested hills and tiny hidden valleys, skim over shining seas and deep inland lakes, look face to face with craggy cliff tops and float unconcernedly over treacherous bogs and quicksand. In the process, they open up the beauty of nature to photographers and all who view the results.

As RC drones are becoming increasingly affordable, the investment of a few hundred dollars can establish a nature photographer. For example, with a durable quadcopter such as a Parrot AR Drone 2.0, you can reach up to 400 feet. With good achievable height and the built-in powerful camera, you can take stunning HD photos and videos of nature.

If you prefer a more powerful front-facing approach to nature, numerous RC drones have powerful 1080p front and rear-facing cameras. This allows you to capture the beauty of nature from afar, using a number of filters and photography styles such as fish-eye. Either way, a good drone and built-in camera will allow you to capture nature's best kept secrets for up to 25 minutes.

For the best nature photos, be sure to do as much advance planning as possible. View the terrain on Google Earth and check for any attractions on Flickr. Once your quadcopter is flying, shoot fast and often. Don't be afraid to shoot wide; you can always crop later.

Formal Events

Traditional milestones in life from weddings to proms to family re-unions can be remembered differently when aerial photography using RC drones is in play.

Classic pictures are emerging of graduation ceremonies, friends' weddings, christenings, promotion parities and annual dinners with drone photography. The opportunities for taking aerial photos of formal events are endless.

In the United States alone, there are more than 2.5 million weddings (read photographic opportunities) a year. Just as the videographer found his or her place beside the photographer, so will the aerial photographer in the future. When something special is going on in life, people want to see it from all angles.

With a relatively small drone and a few battery packs, you can capture stunning aerial photos of weddings. With most RC drone manufacturers providing separate hulls for indoor and outdoor use, you will be able to effortlessly capture precious moments with a greater number of people and from different angles.

For example, with an indoor RC quadcopter, you can take pictures of the entire party from the top, capturing every element of any formal event. With a front-facing camera drone, you can fly through events and take pictures as you go, or even record videos. This allows you to capture moments without anyone noticing the camera is on focused them, resulting in natural event pictures.

Best of all, it makes for fun photography. Not only do you capture aerial pictures in stunning HD, flying a drone at a formal event such as a dinner is fun.

Sporting Events

Whether it is your child's first football game or a championship baseball match, recording these events can be difficult because you may not have the right view. You can either choose to stand for the entire match at an ideal location or you can choose the safer and better alternative and use an RC drone.

An RC drone with a 3-axis gyrometer can take stable pictures and videos of the entire match from above. By controlling the RC drone to be above your head, you can autopilot it to record the entire match without ever moving an inch. Of course, you will have to switch batteries, at maximum, after 25 minutes.

If you love go-kart racing, an RC drone can help you keep a watchful eye over your practice runs and even record them. This allows you to gain feedback on your driving, permitting you to adjust your style before the big event.

If you are part of the school's media club and you need pictures of the grounds or an overview of the entire field with the players, you can easily capture it with an RC quadcopter's vertical camera.

Filmmaking

RC drones have been used for several years to make some of the most interesting videos around, both for the big screen and your average YouTube videos. Their use makes plenty of sense, often because it eliminates the need for a big towering camera or high camera positioning.

Filmmaking has always been a hot topic when it comes to RC drones, and I really mean hot. Do you know why? Because drones are completely exempted from normal regulations in Hollywood. If they can do it, why can't the average filmmaker?

For small filmmakers, getting a wide angle or overhead shot involves either climbing into a tree (so to speak) or using a lifter. This is either dangerous or expensive. A drone is an inexpensive way to get such shots.

Fortunately, since last September when the FAA said they would open the air for filmmakers, the topic got hotter. However, only six companies were allowed to use drones for filmmaking. But all things change and our time will surely come.

If you have been following news about RC drones for a while you may be aware of the work of Raphael Pirker, the businessmen who used an RC drone to film footage for a University of Virginia Medical Center advertisement.

For his filmmaking adventures, the FAA fined Raphael $10,000. However, in March 2014, the proposed fine was revoked. He won because the FAA hadn't created rules and regulations for model aircrafts.

Today, most model aircrafts are known as "drones" and thus you need to be careful. For now, commercial applications carry a fine and are not recommended. Your choice to do so is solely up to you.

As such, you are free to use your RC drones to make your own home movies, non-profit family-filled series and YouTube videos. Again, you cannot make profits from them; otherwise it will be regarded as a commercial application.

Movies

When it comes to expensive blockbuster movies, they pull out all the stops in order to make the movie a hit. This includes using drones, planes and helicopters for aerial footage. Rather than choosing a helicopter or plane for aerial footage, you can use your RC drone to make movies and gain aerial footage.

While an RC drone may not be able to fly as high as a plane or offer the combination of stability and height a helicopter can, it is an affordable way to gain aerial footage.

If you have a quadcopter with a front and/or back-facing camera, filming your movies should be a simple task.

If your quadcopter is equipped with a vertical camera, you can capture top-down footage as well.

YouTube Videos

Whether it is for a small school project or for personal fun, video series are great to make, watch and upload to YouTube. Rather than use regular camera techniques to record your video, you can use an RC drone. While I know a tripod works great for stabilization, I doubt a tripod can help you reach as high as an RC drone can.

Not only does it work similarly to a regular camera, it also allows you to take footage from angles higher off the ground. Most importantly, it lets you have plenty of fun with your RC drone as well. Because, let's face it, using a drone is already fun, and using it to make your YouTube videos is even better. You can even use your drone to make great chase scenes as well.

What makes RC drones the perfect filming tool for your YouTube videos is their low cost. Maintaining expensive filming equipment for short YouTube videos is costly, but maintaining an RC drone does not always have to be. Sure, your drone may crash, damaging the equipment, but the fixes for the drone are more affordable than an HD camera. Moreover, the parts are easily available and interchangeable, at least more than a good HD camera.

Real Estate

Current estimates suggest the American real estate industry generates well over $200 billion in revenue every year and employs more than one million individuals. However, as any real estate agent and company knows, securing a real estate deal is never an easy task. In fact, it is often time consuming. This is especially true for smaller companies and agents.

It usually involves uploading numerous quality pictures of the home onto the Internet so potential buyers or tenants can see the home. If they like the home, they will schedule to meet you there so you can give them a tour.

Aerial photography taken with drones is growing in demand. Recognizing that 9 out of 10 buyers start their home searches online, industry officials are cognizant of the reality that pictures really do mean thousands of words in this case.

Even though hiring a UAV photographer is not legal yet, the practice is going on behind the scenes as people wait for the laws to change.

For many real estate firms handling higher end homes, the demand is keen. They know that a luxury home in a beautifully landscaped setting gives people an immediate sense of what it would be like to live there. They understand that to sell property worth millions of dollars, people have to have a sense of how it feels and looks in perspective to the neighborhood around it.

Able to navigate tight spaces and capture pictures photographers normally cannot, an RC drone can be the very thing you need to help save time, attract the right buyers and secure deals faster.

RC drones can be used for a variety of purposes, including:

- Capturing the right pictures

- Giving online tours

- Creating an interesting sales video

When the FAA regulations change this is expected to be a mega-growth industry. In the meantime, some photographers are getting around the regulations by taking the photos for free with their quadcopters, and then charging to edit them. It's a fine line that many are willing to walk for the commercial benefits.

Exterior Property Pictures

When it comes to taking pictures of property, almost any photographer can capture pictures of a home's exterior while standing and "point-clicking" with a camera. However, if you want truly remarkable pictures that will attract buyers or tenants, an RC drone can help you.

Equipped with both front-facing and vertical cameras, you can take pictures from a distance and above the property, allowing you to capture even more of the property in each picture.

When it comes to taking pictures of the home, you can take elevated vertical pictures as well with your RC drone. This will allow you to show your potential buyers or tenants an entire picture of your home's exterior in a single shot.

Online Tours and Sales Videos

While many potential home buyers and tenants have the time to visit a home for a tour, many others do not. Moreover, giving so many tours is exhausting and will eventually become frustrating. In fact, with the busy schedules many people have they may not have the time to visit your home at all and will be relying on sales videos and virtual tours.

With an RC drone, you can create online tours and videos and upload them to your website. This allows you to film one entire video of both the outside and inside of the home, giving your potential buyers or tenants a tour of the home without ever coming there.

Potential buyers are very attracted to videos taken with cameras mounted on drones. That is because there is an authenticity to them: what you see literally is what you get.

When you view a file of still pictures for a virtual tour, you are usually viewing a number of carefully captured pictures that are often photo shopped. Evidently, this makes the home look better than it is.

With a single video, you know you are seeing the house in all its glory as it really is. This makes it a more accurate tour. Moreover, you do not have to click and load hundreds of pictures. All you have to do is let the video buffer, and simply "seek" back to the parts you wanted to see.

Moreover, only those interested after the online tour will contact you for a proper tour. This increases the chances of closing a deal.

The same effectiveness can be achieved when making a sales video by drone. In the past, anyone could create a simple slideshow of pictures of their home but it was static and often missed the ambiance of the home. With an RC drone, you can create a special sales video that combines both your drone's video with a descriptive voice-over. The impact can be stunning.

Unlike regular sales videos, an RC drone is very stable and can move fluidly in and out of rooms. This also helps you record a shake-free sales video that will help you sell your home.

Package Delivery

A few decades ago when you wanted a package delivered to your home, you ended up having to walk or drive somewhere yourself to pick it up and bring it home.

Gradually times changed and people looked for other options so they could proceed with their other work and have someone else do this chore.

Slowly, the US postal service took over in 1971 and became the easiest way to have a package delivered, and it is still one of the most popular methods used. However, it does cost money and often it is not ideal for fast deliveries over short distances in a city.

If you need to deliver packages over short distances without leaving your home and you do not want to pay postage for it, the solution is simple: RC drones. Equipped with the right carrier, you can convert any simple RC drone into a package delivery system that will make your life easier than ever.

Using an RC drone for package delivery is a very interesting application. Unlike the applications above, this only has two: recreational and commercial. Moreover, considering the current limitations imposed by the Federal Aviation Authority (FAA), the use of RC drones for commercial delivery is banned. However, there are indications that this may change in the future.

When it comes to package delivery for your own personal recreational purposes, I highly recommend you purchase an accessory known as a drone basket. This is a small basket that hangs from the underside of your drone. Although it may feel light and flimsy at first, it is strong enough for many of the applications below.

Sending Items Throughout Your Home

When nobody in your family wants to detach themselves from their gadgets and go get some snacks, why not send some goodies to them? With a powerful and affordable indoor RC drone, you can attach a package of chips and deliver it to any member of the family. To make your life simpler, use the drone basket I mentioned. However, there are only certain things you can place in it.

This allows mothers everywhere to quickly send anyone almost anything from the fridge or pantry without climbing the stairs. Best of all, controlling an RC drone is fun and delivering food with the drone makes it even better.

Oftentimes you need to send small items throughout the house. For example, someone may ask for their car keys or watch. If you are having a barbeque, you may need to grab some oil from the kitchen and bring it back outside.

Rather than walking across the hallway or back inside your home, use your RC drone. Attach a small clip or basket and simply send items across your home with ease. While you can walk across the hallway to hand your brother the USB, it is just more fun using an RC drone.

Delivering Packages

Need to send pictures or files over to your friend living across the street? Don't worry about slipping into something decent just to deliver a file. Use your RC drone instead!

With the right RC drone, you can send small packages over quickly. For example, if you want to send your flash drive over to your friend's home, simply place the camera into the drone's basket and secure it tight. Once you do, fly it over to your neighbor's home and once they take it out, fly your drone back. You could go over there and deliver it separately but where's the fun in that?

This small act in your neighborhood is nothing compared to the prospects for package delivery by drones on a large commercial scale, however.

Consider that people working at Amazon.com more than a year ago had to walk miles on every shift, going around different aisles in their massive warehouses to find the items online customers had ordered, pick them up by hand, and bring them to a central location for packing and shipping.

Today that task is done by 15,000 robot drones that zoom about the company's largest warehouses to deliver the toys, books and other products to the employees who pack them.

Even though public attention has focused on Amazon.com's public announcement that they would like to test delivering packages with drones and they are currently doing so in countries where regulations allow it, more and more firms are making use of drones in their own warehouses. Inside the warehouse walls they do not have to deal with the FAA regulations, they don't have to worry about the weather and they aren't in danger of flying into the path of manned aircraft.

The Chinese conglomerate Alibaba recently tested drone delivery by sending little bags of ginger tea from a warehouse on the outskirts of Beijing to the China World Trade Center. The drones, which were also being tested in Shanghai and Guangzhou, had a 2.2 pound capacity and a 6.2 mile range

The U.S. Marine Corps program in Afghanistan has delivered packages using two unmanned helicopters, and delivery giant UPS has acknowledged it is testing delivery by means of parcel-carrying drones. Rather than getting mired in the regulations that so far make door-to-door delivery unlikely, they are using the drones to take parcels from airports to warehouses in remote areas.

Security

Whether it is in the first or the 21st century, security has always been a paramount concern to both individuals and businesses. From selecting a powerful leader for a village or the right technology to protect an entire country, people want the right protection decisions made.

From a small to a large operation, RC drones can help you improve your security infrastructure both in terms of size and efficiency. While drones cannot be used to replace security personnel, they can be used as an extension, helping them to perform their jobs better.

For example, while a drone cannot replace a security patrol officer, it can help them scan areas ahead of them, ensuring they do not have to get up unless something seems out of order.

While it is true that commercial applications of drones even for security purposes is permissible at this time, as indicated at the beginning, changes are coming. Already some jurisdictions are making changes and the FAA is expected to work their adjustments to regulations through the system in the coming months.

In Denver Colorado, a new drone bill is in the works that allows law enforcement agencies to use drones in a number of ways. Some examples are given below.

Security Patrols

Security patrol officers walk along and scrutinize large areas. At times, they look through cameras to see what areas require attention and other times they patrol the area either way.

Advance security patrols done with drones gives the officers the ability to cover up to twice as much area as they did before. This is because the drone can scan one area while the patrol officer scans another. This allows them to cover the areas the drone did not cover. In fact, used efficiently, it can help alert guards to problems faster and more accurately than before.

Meanwhile the Georgia Department of Transportation has applied for and received a $75,000 grant from the Federal Highway Administration to study whether or not drones could be used to inspect roads and bridges, to alert officials to traffic jams and accidents, and to survey land with laser mapping. If drones are found to be successful in highway monitoring the results will be stupendous, considering there are almost four million miles of highways across the United States alone.

Alert Detection

From a small rat to a huge person, a variety of objects will trigger security alerts in any system. Sometimes these alerts are false, but they can also be very real and exceptionally dangerous.

Rather than being caught off-guard, security personnel can swoop into action with an RC drone and see if the alert truly is from a real threat or not. While security cameras work well, they can easily be tampered with, and their range and swing time makes them susceptible to human trickery.

With an RC drone, you do not have to become a possible distraction. Simply fly your RC drone over to view the trigger.

Chases

Unlike your average security guard, anyone intruding on your premises has an exit strategy in mind and knows how to get away from you and your business or residence quickly. In case of an intrusion, a chase usually develops and often ends in the intruder escaping. This is usually because the security officer chasing the intruder loses sight of them. This problem can be easily overcome by using an RC drone.

The average quadcopter is able to fly at an average of 16 feet per second, allowing it to be a good backup for burglary chases. In case an intruder begins to run away, you can activate your RC drone and give chase. As such, you can continue to monitor them from above, ensuring you do not lose sight of them.

More than just chasing them, the onboard camera can capture footage of the chase and therefore can easily capture a picture of the intruder or capture their face on screen. As such, even if the chase fails and the intruder cannot be caught, their face will at least be captured.

Construction and Energy Industry Monitoring

When it comes to both the construction and energy industries, a range of different hardware, software, human skills and labor is used to perform a multitude of tasks. From surveying sites to analyzing structures and damage, there is plenty to do. While a combined effort does help expedite these processes, the sheer number of individuals and technology used increases the price of construction and energy.

Take the construction industry for example. The use of multiple engineers to assess a construction site is costly, but the task can sometimes be outsourced to RC drones. Just as they assist security personnel, quadcopters that are capable of carrying high-resolution cameras and special sensors can be used to keep track of big projects.

Here is a closer look at all the uses of RC drones in the construction industry.

Site Surveys

Before a tract of land can be used for construction, it needs to be surveyed properly and then tested for its usability. However, this task usually requires numerous individuals to survey large tracts of land. This task can easily be completed by using RC drones.

Quadcopters carrying cameras can make recordings of the construction site, and these can be sent to head offices miles from the location. Many drones run on software that can make 3D layouts as well. With a bird's eye view, architects and engineers can view the entire scene as it is without hiring expensive helicopters to move personnel to the area.

Structural Analysis

Structural analysis plays an important part in the construction of any building, both during and afterwards. The analysis enables engineers to determine just how strong the building is and if it needs additional support. This is a time-consuming task, especially when it comes to measuring angles and monitoring structural integrity. Fortunately, structural analysis can be made easier using RC drones.

Quadcopters can be equipped with a number of different cameras and sensors that allow engineers to use them to perform a structural analysis. As well, pieces of sensitive equipment can be attached to the drone and flown to higher floors to perform a remote analysis, eliminating the need for the engineer to walk up multiple floors.

Damage Analysis

Similar to structural analysis, an RC drone can be used to analyze the damage of any building. Whether it is during construction or after completion, drones can easily access areas others may be unable to reach and thus safely illustrate the damage sustained.

Some companies are using drones to monitor power lines, inspect gas pipelines or oil lines, detect malfunctioning solar panels and check wind turbines for defects or damage.

In an interview published April 21, 2014, Michael Blades, an analyst who studies the UAV industry for the research firm Frost & Sullivan, told reporter Todd Woody of *The New York Times* that drones can do pretty much anything an energy company doesn't want to send people to do.

One of the largest installers of solar panels in the United States is testing drones to detect malfunctioning solar panels. The process appears to be effective to date, since the panels generate a particularly recognizable heat signature as they fail.

A Canadian firm has reportedly dispatched drones to search for cracks in wind turbine blades. Quadcopters equipped with thermal cameras to scan oil pipelines in Alaska and check for structural weaknesses.

The UAVs used in the construction and energy industry tend to be smaller than a big drone used by the military. They are small quadcopters that can synced to 3-D printers and open-source software. Some of the models currently being tested can actually fly alone guided by their GPS system, a camera and a solar sensor. Then the ground station uses its own sensors coupled with a radio signal to signal the drone to return. Once back, its data and battery are removed and new batteries installed and it is ready to go again.

Some companies are currently testing drones to detect protected wildlife that might wander onto a solar power installation or wind farm. One company uses the drone to scare off birds that are flying too close to a wind turbine. The U.S. Geological Survey has also been testing a small drone carrying a camera to experiment if it could be used to make accurate counts of endangered sand hill cranes.

Education

Education is a big area that needs more focus on both the state and federal levels. According to surveys, an increasing number of children find regular classroom lectures boring and monotonous. The use of interactive software and games has proven to make classroom learning more fun.

Believe it or not, education is a major area of use for RC drones. Not only can they make learning more fun, they can facilitate more interactive lectures. They can enable teachers to show students areas of the world around them they may not be able to see otherwise.

For example, kindergarteners are always fascinated with the world around them. However, in a classroom environment, they have little exposure to the outside world. RC drones can bridge that gap and help teach them about their surroundings in a very different way.

This also means that teachers can prepare their own interactive lectures using their own information rather than information from a text book. They can record videos, take children to the sky using the drone's camera and open their minds like never before. Here is a closer look at how RC drones can be used in the field of education.

Robotics

The subject of robotics is both vast and incredibly interesting. With almost every task becoming autonomous or requiring the aid of a machine or smart technology, it is important for students to understand the world of robotics.

While they may not be million dollar life-saving robots, RC drones show some of the basic concepts of robotics, mathematics, programming and physics. This includes speed, velocity, air pressure, programming functions, trajectory, weight limits, drag and more.

Since RC drones are affordable, especially the smaller ones, they can be pulled apart and pieced together quickly and easily, showing students the world of robotics from within the classroom.

In fact, by using an RC drone, teachers can impart knowledge about concepts in areas such as robotics, mathematics, programming and physics. For example: "Knowing the weight and acceleration of the drone, how much force will it exert on liftoff and how long will it take to reach a height of X feet?" As a result, students learn the concepts of multiple subjects from a single piece of affordable equipment.

Some educational facilities are so fascinated with the future of drones and how they will impact our world that they make them part of the curriculum. In 2013, for example, the College of the North Atlantic became the first higher education facility in Canada to take its journalism program to the skies. As part of its photojournalism course, the college offered instruction in drone journalism complete with remote controlled quadcopters to capture images and data. Instructor Jeff Ducharme said in a news release at the time that journalism is changing rapidly as we search for new and different ways to get information to people, and drone journalism is an exciting part of that trend.

Pennsylvania State University was one of the first higher education institutions in the United States to apply for FAA for permission to have UAVs for academic research purposes but they were refused. Professor Jack Langelaan of the facility's aerospace engineering department wanted the drones so his students could study the flight patterns of albatrosses and other flying birds that travel long distances.

Interactive Sessions

In 2013, high-schoolers in Austin, Texas, were allowed to fly quadcopters, rovers and robotic arms in the classroom to trigger their interest in math and science. The successful program was part of President Barack Obama's "Educate to Innovate" program designed to close the gap between the students' interest and these essential subjects.

RC drones can quickly and easily change the way you impart knowledge through interactive sessions. For example, if you are creating a lecture about the biology of the world around you, try incorporating a video of your drone's "fly-through" of a nearby flower field. This will enable you to not only tell your students about the biology around them, but show them as well. Best of all, since you recorded the footage, you do not have to worry about finding the right free content.

Adventure Stories

The world is full of fun and adventure and your students know this as well. However, until they go out into the world and use their minds in more creative ways, they will be unable to imagine all these stories.

With an RC drone camera, you can stream a video of a popular outdoor attraction in your area to your students and show them the world from a different angle. Looking down on a sight gives you a perspective that you simply cannot appreciate when you walk through it at ground level. You can ask them what they saw on the flight and even to write about a story about it. Did it look more impressive or less impactful from the air? Were the dimensions of the attraction deceiving when viewed from a new angle? Did it look as beautiful or more beautiful from the air? This not only makes learning fun but nourishes a student's creativity.

Recreational Games

By now it is clear that RC drones have plenty of different uses. Some of them make your life easier while some make it more interesting. In essence, however, RC drones are primarily meant to be used for recreational fun. They were made for you to fly in your local clubs or designated fly zones.

You may not want to fly drones much for the purposes of construction, real estate, education, security, filming and aerial photography. You may prefer to use your drones for simple uses such as racing, simulation battles, simple flying and making fun videos.

This helps you make full use for your drone and relax while doing so. Moreover, flying a drone can be a group activity that your family can enjoy as well.

Racing

While there are certain proximity regulations regarding drones, that does not mean you cannot race them with a friend. You can race to see who reaches a height of 400 feet first, gets to a checkpoint before the other or completes a lap before the other.

Building and Modifying

Racing your RC drones is great but building and modifying them, for some, is even better. You can continuously upgrade their battery, design, rotors, parts, camera and accessories to help you create the most creative drone around. Although a rather simple application, it really is fun.

You slowly build and customize your own drone, piecing together the ultimate radio-controlled UAV. You can show it off at your local hobbyist or RC drone club as well.

Simulation Racing and Battles

Technology has come a long way over the past decade and I do not mean in just RC drones. Simulation and augmented reality is working to make your life even better and your activities more fun. When it comes to RC drones, many manufacturers include an augmented reality version of simulation battles in their app.

For example, with Parrot's AR Drone, right from the beginning the attraction wasn't just that it was an RC drone. Instead, it was a fascinating new kind of virtual gaming device. The company designed several augmented reality game apps, most of them multi-player for added fun. These air combat or racing games were AR overlays which permitted users to fire virtual missiles at each other.

In other words, you can be flying your drone like normal and the software creates scenarios on screen and simulated races or even aerial battles. These fun features make RC drones great toys.

Fishing

Fishing is a relaxing activity that most of us love and enjoy. It involves a weekend or day of peace and tranquility where you and Mother Nature are together for a few magnificent hours. Whether you take the fish home or fish for sport (catch and release), recreational fishing can be made better with quadcopters.

They can also help with professional fishing. For 221 million people around the world, fishing is their only source of livelihood. Locating schools of fish and the right fishing spot is not easy without expensive equipment.

Many professional companies use very expensive equipment and technology such as seafloor maps, radio waves and even sonar (audio and visual) to track fish. If you do not have the money for such expensive equipment, an RC drone is a great way to overcome such a problem.

An RC drone can make life simpler for both the recreational and commercial fisherman. An RC drone can help you:

- Locate fish

- Find the right fishing spot

- Take great pictures

Locating Schools of Fish

If you are a commercial fisher, one of the biggest difficulties is finding a relatively large school of fish. If you own an expensive fishing boat, you likely have sonar technology attached to it. If you do not, locating schools of fish can be time consuming. You can locate schools of fish better and faster with an RC drone.

When equipped with both a camera and professional sonar, the drone will help you locate schools of fish easily. The sonar will be able to tell you how deep the fish are while the camera can give you a visual cue of where you need to move your boat. This is great for lower to medium-end fishers.

Finding the Right Fishing Spot

If you love fishing on the weekend, I understand that finding the perfect fishing spot can be a little frustrating at times. There are spots where you probably cast your line and get no bites. It may not happen every time, but it is frustrating when it does. An RC drone can make your life easier by helping you visually locate the perfect fishing spot.

With an RC drone, you can visually locate the perfect fishing spot from above. The best thing is that you can do this before ever casting your line or placing your boat in the water. Launch your drone in the air and survey for the right fishing spot. Perhaps the fish are biting 200 feet away from your usual spot today. The best part about an RC drone when you go fishing is that any type of camera can be used on the drone.

For example, if you use a front-facing camera to locate a fishing spot, you will be able to fly the drone over water and locate different spots. On the other hand, you can also fly your RC quadcopters vertically and take an overall view of the water under the drone and visually locate the perfect fishing spot.

In fact, this makes it a great tool when you are visiting a new fishing spot. Before you decide to visit the spot for the weekend, you can use the drone to scope out the nearby waters for schools of fish. After all, wild fish never stay in the same place for long.

Capturing Beautiful Pictures of Your Fishing Experience

When you travel to your favorite spot to enjoy a good day of fishing, you will likely want to capture HD pictures of your catches and the beautiful area around you. Do not be the average recreational fisherman who just takes a picture of themselves and the fish; be different.

With an RC drone, you can take an aerial picture of yourself, your catch and the area around you. If you choose to take a vertical picture with all your catch in your boat, you can take quite a beautiful picture.

Farming

Creating more than 751,000 jobs and accounting for over $374 billion in revenue, the United States agricultural industry is huge and continuously growing. With so much to do on any farm, any kind of technological assistance is welcome, since the sheer amount of physical labor needed is daunting.

Unfortunately, this is not always a feasible option, especially if farmers have few financial resources available. As a result, farmers choose to handle almost every new task themselves. This could include crop analysis, cattle herding, and even package delivery.

While they will manage it somehow, there are relatively easier ways to handle these increases in work. One of the easiest solutions is to hire more farmhands. Unfortunately, if you run a small farm, this is not usually possible.

Rather than increasing your own workload and walking more miles on your farm than you should, you can use an RC drone. If it does not make sense now, do not worry as it will very soon.

Certain tasks require you to move throughout the farm. In the heat of summer, this can be very tiring and often dangerous. A technological helper in the form of a quadcopter can be beneficial . For example, picture a farmer five fields away from his house who suddenly discovers an unfamiliar insect attacking a plant. He wants to capture a specimen for identification and testing, but doesn't have his portable science kit with him. He calls his house, gets someone there to put a specimen bottle and tweezers into a drone, and it is sent to him immediately, without having to leave the spot and try to locate it again.

Here is a quick look at the different ways you can use your fun-filled RC drone on your farm.

Cattle Herd Management

A recent article by agricultural law authority Todd Janzen in ▢*ro*▢*res*▢ *s*▢▢*e* ▢*attle*▢*an* envisions the day a drone can fly out to a rancher's pasture to check on the cattle herd. The drone reports back that the herd is all accounted for except for one steer that is lying down about 1,000 feet away from the others and looks sick. The drone sends the exact GPS coordinates of the steer to the rancher, who dispatches a person to check the animal and possibly save its life.

When diseased cattle can cost a rancher his year, identifying sick animals is of paramount importance and drones can be useful in this regard. Animals in the early stages of illness or stress emit a degree of heat that can be detected by a drone carrying a thermal camera.

Crop Analysis

Crop analysis is an exacting task. It involves going around the farm and looking at samples of your crops to ensure none are growing below your expectations. Rather than walk around all day analyzing your crops, why not use your RC drone?

From the comfort of a shaded area, you can fly your drone and pick out crops that need closer study and analysis. Diseased plants, like animals, also heat up in the early stages of illness or stress, and these too can be detected by flying drones containing thermal cameras.

With the drone's speed and mobility, a farmer can receive up-to-date data on crop areas daily, despite the distance that needs to be covered. This makes farming less labor intensive and analysis more accurate, since issues with crops can be determined in earlier stages before whole fields are impacted.

Final Words

We have explored a number of areas in which drones will change our world forever, and even as this book wraps up, enterprising quadcopter lovers are finding new ways to delight and intrigue us.

Darwin Aerospace, a research lab, has actually built the world's first Burrito Bomber, a drone with an HTML 5web app. Customers can order Mexican food and track the drone's delivery in real time. They go outside when it's time and the drone drops the burrito to them in a parachute, and then it flies back home.

In England, a sushi restaurant, YO! Sushi, uses a drone with two built-in cameras teamed with an iPad to deliver food to customers. Locals have dubbed it the iTray.

In the United States, Domino's Pizza announced a couple of years ago that it is studying how the firm could use drones to deliver pizza.

More and more recreational athletes are using drones to take pictures of themselves running in marathons or hiking up mountains.

In 2013, the Golf Channel experimented with drone photography during the Arnold Palmer Invitational Tournament.

We are clearly just scratching the surface of how our creative world will make use of drones and quadcopters in the future, especially if some of the serious commercial restrictions are eased. In fact, this year "The Drone Prize" was launched, a competition that invites amateurs to come up with new ways to use drones to improve society.

Contest director Edward Colson said in a press release that drones can be a great benefit to society when used properly. He said he was aware that people have concerns, but he feels they will be eased if they can see how drones can be used in positive ways.

Among the entries submitted this year was a team whose members equipped a UAV to assist in search and rescue operations, and a proposal to show how video shots from a drone could help authorities detect burnt-out streetlights in Greenville, N.C.

In this guide, however, I hope your perception of what they can do and how they can infiltrate your world has been broadened, and that you have picked up the idea that they really are great fun.

Whether you are a photographer, filmmaker, real estate agent, security or construction company, farmer, fisherman, educator, child, teenager or adult, RC drones can be used in more ways than any of us can currently imagine.

Now I pass my passion on to you and believe that you will love using RC drones as much as I do. I hope you will be able to find plenty more uses than what I have told you. I encourage you to be creative and use a number of RC drone additions such as baskets, clips, and strings to enjoy your drone even more.

I really hope you enjoyed this eBook and will enjoy RC drones as much as I do, share my passion and take it to new heights. For all those eagerly awaiting commercial applications, hopefully the FAA will begin to ease into the field soon. After all, there is much to be gained for the economy if we can tap into this estimated $1.7 billion industry.

Got a second?

Thank you for purchasing and reading my book! I hoped you liked it and was able to gather some valuable information.

Can I ask a quick favor?

If you liked this book, I would really appreciate if you could take a minute to leave a review on Amazon. I love getting feedback from my readers and read all of my reviews!

Sincerely,

Eric Hall

www.ingramcontent.com/pod-product-compliance
Lightning Source LLC
Chambersburg PA
CBHW071011180526
45168CB00003B/1380